D0853275

Other books in this series:
A Feast of After Dinner Jokes   A Bouquet of Wedding Jokes
A Portfolio of Business Jokes   A Spread of Over 40s Jokes
A Round of Golf Jokes   A Binge of Diet Jokes
A Romp of Naughty Jokes   A Tankful of Motoring Jokes

Published in the USA in 1993 by Exley Giftbooks
Published in Great Britain in 1993 by Exley Publications Ltd

Cartoons © Bill Stott 1993
Copyright © Helen Exley 1993
ISBN 1-85015-403-1

Series Editor: Helen Exley
Editor: Elizabeth Cotton.

Cover designed by Pinpoint Design Company
Typeset by Delta, Watford. Printed in Hungary

Exley Publications Ltd, 16 Chalk Hill, Watford, Herts WD1 4BN, United Kingdom.
Exley Giftbooks, 359 East Main Street, Suite 3D, Mount Kisco, NY 10549, USA.

Acknowledgements: The publishers gratefully acknowledge permission to reprint copyright material. They
would be pleased to hear from any copyright holders not here acknowledged.
Extracts from *Murphy's Law* and *Murphys Law Bk II* © 1977 & 1980 by Arthur Bloch, reprinted by permission of
Methuen London; extracts from *The Wit's Dictionary* by Colin Bowles, *The World's Best Cricket Jokes* by Ernest
Forbes and *Cricket Widows* by Noel Ford, reprinted by kind permission of Angus and Robertson (a division of
Harper Collins Publishers Ltd.); extracts from *Heroic Failures* and *The Return of Heroic Failures* by Stephen Pile,
reprinted by permission of Rogers, Coleridge & White Ltd.; extracts from ". . . And Finally" by Martyn Lewis
reproduced by permission of Hutchinson; extracts from *Great Sporting Fiascos* reprinted by permission of
Robson Books; extracts from *Stay Fit and Healthy Until You're Dead* by Dave Barry, reprinted by permission of
Rodale Press; extract from *The Public Speaker's Bible* by Stuart Turner, reprinted by permission of Harper
Collins; extracts from *The Random House Book of Jokes and Anecdotes* by Joe Claro, reprinted by permission of
Random House Inc.; extract from *Just Say a Few Words* by Bob Monkhouse, reprinted by permission of Random
House UK Ltd.; extract from *Pass the Port Again* reprinted by permission of Brann Direct Marketing Ltd.; extract
from *A Sailor's Dictionary* by Henry Beard and Roy McKie, reprinted by permission of Workman Publishing;
extracts from *1,001 Great Sports Jokes* by Jeff Rovin, reprinted by permission of Signet.

—A KNOCKOUT OF—
SPORTS
· JOKES ·

EXLEY
MT. KISCO, NEW YORK · WATFORD, UK

THE PERILS OF SPECTATING

"Whenever I go to a ball game I always get the same seat - between the hot dog vendor and his best customer."

*

"In 1908, the England-Wales rugby match was played at Bristol in thick fog. Reports of the match tell how every time a player scored, one of the team cautiously made his way to the side of the pitch to tell the press - and the crowd."

from *Great Sporting Fiascos*

*

"The seat beside Jim at the Redskins playoff game was empty, so Jim said to the man on the other side, 'Pretty incredible to have a no-show at a game like this.'

The man said, 'That's my wife's seat.'

'I see,' said Jim. 'She sick?'

'No. She's dead.'

'Oh,' said Jim. 'Couldn't you find a friend or relative to come with you?'

'Nope,' said the man. 'They're all at her funeral.'"

JEFF ROVIN, from *1001 Great Sports Jokes*

Moser's Law of Spectator Sports:

Exciting play occurs only while you are watching the scoreboard or out buying a hot dog.

ARTHUR BLOCH, from *Murphy's Law*

*

"OK – AWAY YOU GO – AND WATCH OUT FOR THIS NEW GUY
THEY'VE GOT . . ."

What Is A Coach?

"A football coach is a person who is willing to lay down *your* life for the good of the team."

ANON

*

"A football coach is a man whose job is to predict what will happen on Sunday ... then explain, on Monday, why it didn't."

JEFF ROVIN, from *1001 Great Sports Jokes*

*

"In the first-ever World Cup, the trainer of the American soccer team set an example which no other has yet managed to equal. In the 1930 semi-final Argentina had just scored a disputed goal against the USA. Shouting abuse at the referee as he travelled, our fellow dashed out to tend an injured player.

The 80,000 crowd roared with approval as he ran on to the pitch, threw down his medical bag, broke a bottle of chloroform and anaesthetized himself.

He was carried off by his own team.

STEPHEN PILE, from *The Return of Heroic Failures*

*

DUFFERS UNITE!

"'When you were at college, what position did you play?' the small girl asked her father.

'I was a back.'

'Full back or half back.'

'Drawback,' came the reply."

P. BROWN

*

He had a bad day in the field, dropping six catches, and now as he sat huddled in the dressing room he could feel a cold coming on.

"I think I've caught a cold," he muttered.

"Thank goodness you're able to catch something," grunted the captain.

ERNEST FORBES, from The World's Best Cricket Jokes

*

" ... Frank Sinatra once played eighteen holes with golf pro Arnold Palmer. Afterward, Sinatra asked, 'What do you think of my game?'

'It's not bad,' Palmer said, 'but I still prefer golf.'"

JOE CLARO, from The Random House Book of Jokes

*

"He's never been much of a sportsman. They used to call him Cinderella in the football team... he kept missing the ball."

*

"WELL, THAT'S THAT. I WONDER WHAT IT'LL BE NEXT WEEK?"

The Joys Of Skiing

"This exciting sport got its start as a symptom of mental illness in northern climes such as Norway and Sweden... Americans did very little ski jumping until the television program 'Wide World of Sports' began showing a promotional film snippet in which a ski jumper hurtles off the edge of the chute, completely out of control with various important organs flying out of his body. Fitness buffs saw this and realized that any activity with such great potential for being fatal must be very good for you, so the sport began to catch on."

DAVE BARRY, from *Stay Fit and Healthy until You're Dead*

She tried to learn to ski, but by the time she learned how to stand, she couldn't sit down.

*

"Skiing? Why break my leg at 40 degrees below zero when I can fall downstairs at home?"
COREY FORD

*

"I DON'T THINK I GOT THAT - JUST ASK HIM IF HE'LL DO IT
AGAIN, WOULD YOU, HONEY?"

"No doubt about it . . . every day in every way, my game grows stronger. I saw one enthusiast the other day playing with his racket out of the press. I'll have to try that."

ERMA BOMBECK

*

"PLANNING ON TACKLING MORE THAN TWO SERVES PER POINT?"

" . . . that's what I like about bowling. You can have fun even if you stink, unlike in, say, tennis. Every decade or two I attempt to play tennis, and it always consists of thirty-seven seconds of actually hitting the ball and two hours of yelling, 'Where did the ball go?' . . . With bowling, once you let go of the ball it's no longer your legal responsibility. They have these wonderful machines that find it for you and send it right back."

DAVE BARRY, from *Stay Fit and Healthy until You're Dead*

*

Michehl's Rule for Prospective Mountain Climbers:
> The mountain gets steeper as you get closer.
> Frothinham's corollary:
> The mountain looks closer than it is.

Shendenhelm's Law of Backpacking:
> All trails have more uphill sections than they have level or downhill sections.

ARTHUR BLOCH, from *Murphy's Law*

*

"A group of hikers returning from a day up in the mountains became hopelessly lost in the deep woods. It was almost dark and a sense of panic was growing. 'I thought you said you were the best damn guide in Minnesota.' snapped one of the party.

'Oh, I am,' laughed the guide, 'but I'm pretty sure we're in Manitoba by now.'"

PETER GRAY

*

"OK – HERE COMES ANOTHER ONE – AND THIS TIME I GET

THE HELMET . . ."

UNDERSTANDING THE GAME

"They thought lacrosse was what you found
in la church."

ROBIN WILLIAMS

*

"In winter football is a useful and charming
exercise. It is a leather ball about as big as one's
head, filled with wind. This kick'd about from one to
t'other end in the streets, by him that can get it, and
that is all the art of it."

FRANCOIS MISSON, (1697)

*

"An American takes a foreign friend to a baseball
game. The foreigner is just beginning to get into
cheering batters as they run to first, when a batter
draws a walk.

The foreigner starts to shout, 'Run, boy, run!'

The American with a bemused smile, explains:
'He doesn't have to run; he has four balls.'

His friend stands up and shouts, 'Walk proudly,
boy, walk proudly.'"

from *"And I Quote"*

SILLY GAMES

"Sports is the toy department of human life."

HOWARD COSSELL

*

"I THINK THESE RECORD ATTEMPTS ARE CHEAPENING THE SPORT."

Golf: a game in which you claim the privileges of age, and retain the playthings of childhood.

SAMUEL JOHNSON

*

"It may be the games are silly. But then, so are human beings."

ROBERT LYND

*

"If I ever needed a brain transplant, I'd choose
a sportswriter because I'd want a brain that had
never been used."

NORM VAN BROCKLIN

*

"And no one's ever won The Open three times.
It's been won four times and two times, but never in
its history has it been won three times."

U.S. GOLF COMMENTARY

*

"With the last kick of the game, Bobby
MacDonald scored a header."

ALAN PARRY, Sports commentator

*

"Patrick Tambay's hopes, which were nil before,
are absolutely zero now."

MURRAY WALKER, Sports commentator

*

"For those of you watching who haven't TV sets,
live commentary is on Radio Two."

DAVID COLEMAN, Sports commentator

The Theory & Practice of Gamesmanship or, the Art of Winning Games without Actually Cheating
BOOK TITLE, by STEPHEN POTTER

We beat them five-nothing, and they were lucky to score nothing.

*

"If I hadn't already won three Nationals, I'd think I was fated never to win it."

TIM FORSTER

*

"Serious sport has nothing to do with fair play . . . It is war minus the shooting."

GEORGE ORWELL

*

"I DON'T KNOW WHO HE IS, BUT I DON'T THINK HE'S A CLUB MEMBER . . ."

"NOT EVERYONE CAN BE A BRONZED ADONIS."

THE BODY BEAUTIFUL

It's said that swimming develops poise and grace, but have you seen how a duck walks?

*

"I failed to make the chess team, because of my height."

WOODY ALLEN

*

They may say that walking is a good exercise, but did you ever see a postman as well built as a truck driver?

*

"I was watching sumo wrestling on the television for two hours before I realized it was darts."

HATTIE HAYRIDGE

*

"I try not to break the rules, merely to test their elasticity."

BILL VEECK

*

The true definition of a golfer is one who shouts "Fore", takes five, and puts down a three.

*

Gomez's Law

"If you don't throw it, they can't hit it."

LEFTY GOMEZ

*

"I believe in rules. Sure I do. If there weren't any rules, how could you break them?"

LEO DUROCHER

*

Did you hear about the golfer who cheated so much that when he got a hole-in-one he put down a zero on his score card?

*

"I AGREE – BOXING IS VIOLENT AND DANGEROUS – BUT
LET'S FACE IT – I DON'T THINK YOU ARE GOING
TO HURT ANYBODY . . ."

BOXING CLEVER ...

"I was called 'Rembrandt' Hope in my boxing days, because I spent so much time on the canvas."

BOB HOPE

*

"In February 1977 Mr. Harvey Gartley became the first boxer to knock himself out after 47 seconds of the first round of his first fight before either boxer had landed a punch.

It happened in the regional bantamweight heats of the 15th annual Saginaw Golden Gloves contest in Michigan, when Gartley was matched against Dennis Outlette. Neither boxer had fought in public before. Both were nervous.

Gartley started promisingly and came out of his corner bobbing, weaving and dancing. As the crowd roared them on, Gartley closed in, threw a punch, missed and fell down exhausted. The referee counted him out."

STEPHEN PILE, from *Heroic Failures*

*

Just Give Up!

"If at first you don't succeed - so much for sky diving."

ANON

"TECHNICALLY, THAT'S IMPOSSIBLE . . ."

"YOU'RE NEW TO CLUB COMPETITION, RIGHT?"

My best punch is the rabbit punch...too bad they never let me fight a rabbit.

*

"Jackie Gleason was another entertainer who was an avid golfer. He once introduced his friend Toots Shor to the game, and Shor racked up a miserable 211. After the game, he asked Gleason, 'What do you think I should give the caddy?'

'Your clubs,' Gleason said."

JOE CLARO, from *The Random House Book of Jokes*

*

ATHLETES ANONYMOUS

"Whenever I feel like exercise, I lie down until the feeling passes."

ROBERT M. HUTCHINS

*

"The only reason I would take up jogging is so that I could hear heavy breathing again."

ERMA BOMBECK

*

"Why don't they establish a local branch of 'Athletes Anonymous . . .' When you feel the urge to play 18 holes of golf, a strenuous set of tennis or a tough game of squash, you just ring them up and they send over a chap who will sit with you and drink until the feeling passes."

P. M. RENNEY

*

"I get my exercise acting as a pall-bearer to my friends who exercise."

CHAUNCEY DEPEW

*

"WHY DO I PLAY GOLF? TO KEEP IN SHAPE. HOW ABOUT YOU?"

"THE CLUB VETERAN. HE LIKES TO DO THE CROSSWORD ON THE WAY DOWN."

boxing (n.) picking up your teeth with gloves on.

KIN HUBBARD

*

skiing (n.) whoosh! then walk a mile.

ANON

*

football (n.) running 50 metres to kick a ball behind two goalposts.

Association Football (n.) running 50 metres to hit the ball with your head behind two goalposts.

Australian Rules Football (n.) running 50 metres to hit the other player in the head from behind two goalposts.

Rugby League Football (n.) running 50 metres, getting kicked in the behind, ramming the other player's head into the goalposts and sod the ball.

COLIN BOWLES, from The Wit's Dictionary

"I'm one of the few to ever throw a javelin two hundred yards . . . actually I only threw it one hundred yards. The guy it hit crawled the other hundred."

JOSÉ JIMENIZ (BILL DANA)

*

"When a rugby player yelled as his dislocated shoulder received attention, the nurse pointed out that a woman had just given birth to a baby, with much less fuss. 'Maybe,' said the player, 'but let's see what happens if you try to put it back.'"

STUART TURNER, from *The Public Speaker's Bible*

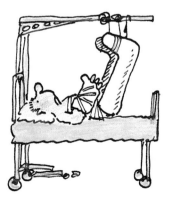

"Did you hear about the former basketball star who became a prizefighter and developed cauliflower naval . . ."

JEFF ROVIN, from *1001 Great Sports Jokes*

*

"I won't mention the name of this particular team we were playing, but at half time we came in, pulled off our socks and began putting iodine on the teeth marks in our legs."

RED GRANGE

ATHLETES 10 – MEDIA 0

Wagner's Law of Sports Coverage:

"When the camera isolates on a male athlete, he will spit, pick or scratch."

ARTHUR BLOCH, from *Murphy's Law Bk 11*

*

"Watch the time - it gives you a good indication of how fast they are running."

RON PICKERING, Sports Commentator

*

"And this line up for the final of the women's 400 metres hurdles includes three Russians, two East Germans, a Pole, a Swede and a Frenchman."

DAVID COLEMAN, Sports Commentator

*

"Bill Toomey, the USA's 1968 Olympic decathlon champion, had one of his most stunning encounters with a feature writer from one of America's biggest newspapers.

'How far can you actually throw the decathlon?'"

from *Great Sporting Fiascos*

"THAT'S A FAST START!"

*"GOSH! ORIENTEERING IS SO EXCITING – THE PLACE WE'RE
AT RIGHT NOW HAS SKULL AND CROSSBONE SYMBOLS
ALL OVER IT!"*

THE ART OF LOSING

Jensen's Law:

Win or lose, you lose.

ARTHUR BLOCH, from Murphy's Law

*

"A veteran golfer was constantly defeated by the 13th hole. That hole always got the better of him, always made him finish up one or two strokes over par. He told his wife, 'When I die, I want to get my own back on that 13th hole if it kills me! Promise me you'll have my ashes scattered all over that damned 13th hole.' And sure enough, when he died, after the funeral, his wife solemnly scattered his ashes all over the fairway – and the wind blew them out of bounds."

BOB MONKHOUSE, from "Just Say a Few Words"

*

What's the best way to stop a runaway horse? Put a bet on it.

*

STRANGE BUT TRUE

"Golf has certainly slowed up considerably at Tuam Golf Club near Galway in the West of Ireland. Players have reported losing a lot of balls - not because of the rough, but because of a large crow. It's carried off dozens of members' balls - on one occasion more than twenty in one day - by snatching them off the course and dropping them out of bounds, and out of reach, in a nearby bog."

MARTYN LEWIS, from *And Finally ...*

*

"Keen to play their annual needle match with Nairobi Harlequins in 1974, the fifteen members of Mombasa Rugby Football Club flew 475 miles to Uganda. During the one-and-a-half-hour journey they passed the no less enthusiastic Harlequins team thirty thousand feet below who were travelling in a fleet of cars to Mombasa. Nine hundred and fifty miles later both teams rang to find out what had happened to the opposition."

STEPHEN PILE, from *The Return of Heroic Failures*

*

"In a club match in Australia a fast bowler delivered what can only be described as a real scorcher. The batsman's trousers burst into flames when the ball hit him on the thigh. It seems he'd left a box of matches in his pocket."

MARTYN LEWIS, from *And Finally ...*

*

"THERE YOU ARE SON – I MENDED THE HOLE IN YOUR BASKET

SO THE BALL WON'T KEEP DROPPING OUT . . ."

Kids Games

Interest your children in bowling. Get them off the streets and into the alleys.

*

"As the ball flew off the sandlot diamond, one kid in the outfield yelled, 'Jeepers! It's a run home!'

The batter yelled, 'You mean, a home run!'

'No, a run home! You smashed somebody's windshield.'"

JEFF ROVIN, from *1001 Great Sports Jokes*

*

"Any American boy can be a basketball star if he grows up, up, up."

BILL VAUGHAN

*

In Fear Of Sport

"Oh God, if there be cricket in heaven, let there also be rain."

SIR ALEC DOUGLAS HOME

*

"I'm afraid I play no outdoor games at all, except dominoes. I have played dominoes outside a French café."

OSCAR WILDE

*

Golf is a lot of walking, broken up by disappointment and bad arithmetic.

*

"Golf is a good walk spoiled."

MARK TWAIN

*

"The greatest dread of all, the dread of games."

JOHN BETJEMAN

*

"Hang gliding, blast baseball, and sod cycling."

ANON

*

"STOP MOANING – YOU SHOULD HAVE GONE BEFORE
WE TOOK OFF . . ."

"MINE!"

ARMED AND DANGEROUS

"When she heard little Nancy cursing during Jumprope, the schoolyard monitor hurried over.

'Now, now,' the woman said, 'you know what happens to little girls who say naughty words!'

'Yes,' said Nancy, 'they grow up and play tennis.'"
JEFF ROVIN, from 1001 Great Sports Jokes

*

Raquet Ball/Squash

"This is a popular sport wherein you and another person go into a white room, close the door, and attempt to injure each other in the eye.
DAVE BARRY, from Stay Fit and Healthy until You're Dead

*

"'Good shot,' 'bad luck,' and 'hell' are the five basic words to be used in a game of tennis, though these, of course, can be slightly amplified."
VIRGINIA GRAHAM

*

"Squash is boxing with rackets."
JONAH BARRINGTON

*

Deal's Law of Sailing:

1. The amount of wind will vary inversely with the number and experience of the people you take on board.

2. No matter how strong the breeze when you leave the dock, once you have reached the furthest point from port the wind will die.

ARTHUR BLOCH, from *Murphy's Law Book II*

*

a yacht (n.) a floating box you throw money into.

*

Sailing (n.) the fine art of getting wet and becoming ill while slowly going nowhere at great expense.

HENRY BEARD & ROY McKIE
from *A Sailor's Dictionary*

*

"HAPPY, DARLING?"

"JUST GO EASY ON THE SQUEEZING – I HAD AN ESPECIALLY

STRONG VEGETABLE CURRY LAST NIGHT."

Rough And Tumble ...

A boy came home after his first football game with a broken nose, a torn ear and three loose teeth, but he couldn't remember who they belonged to.

*

"Then there was the football coach who decided to take a gorilla on tour with his team. So if any of his players got injured, he'd have spare parts."

JEFF ROVIN, from *1001 Great Sports Jokes*

*

"Be kind to animals: Hug a hockey player."

Bumper Sticker

*

When fighting Mike Tyson, there's only one thing more important than presence of mind. Absence of body.

*

Win Or Else

"Ralph Kiner, home run ace for the Pittsburgh Pirates in the days when the team could scarcely win a game, once told this story about the early days of his marriage to former tennis star Nancy Chaffee.

'When I married Nancy,' Ralph said, 'I vowed I'd beat her at tennis some day. After six months, she beat me 6-2. After a year, she beat me 6-4. After we were married a year and a half, I pushed her to 7-5. Then it happened. She had a bad day, and I had a good one, and I beat her 17-15.'

At this point in the story, Kiner was asked if his wife had been sick on that day.

'Of course not!' he said. Then he added, 'Well – she *was* eight months pregnant.'"

JOE CLARO, from *The Random House Book of Jokes*

*

"I'm the best. I just haven't played yet."

MUHAMMAD ALI, when asked about his golf game

*

Ade's Law:

"Anybody can win – unless there's a second entry."

GEORGE ADE

RULES IS RULES

"The devil was continually challenging St. Peter to a game of soccer, but St. Peter refused, until one day while walking around heaven he discovered that quite a number of Irish International footballers had entered the 'pearly gates'.

'Now I'll arrange to play you that soccer game.' said St. Peter. 'How about it?'

'You'll lose,' said the devil, 'you'll lose.'

'Oh, don't be sure,' replied St. Peter. 'We now have in heaven a great number of International soccer stars from which to select a winning team.'

'You'll lose, you'll lose!' repeated the devil.

'What makes you so sure we'll lose?' enquired St. Peter.

'Because,' laughed the devil, 'we have all the referees down here.'"

LORD BLEASE, J.P., from *Pass The Port Again*

*

Stigstad's Law:

When it gets to be your turn, they change the rules.

ARTHUR BLOCH, from *Murphy's Law Bk 11*

SPORT CRAZY

INTERVIEWER: "So, Pam, what are your interests outside tennis?"

PAM SHRIVER: "Well, I run a tennis school . . ."

*

"'Fishing! I can't believe it! You spend all weekend at the lake and then you come home and dream about fishing! Why don't you ever dream about me?'

'What, and miss a bite?'"

E.P.R.

*

"If all the Cricket Widows in the world were laid end to end, their husbands wouldn't notice until the end of the cricket season."

NOEL FORD, from Cricket Widows

*

"My husband's going to leave me if I don't stop my aerobics."

"Oh dear! That's too bad."

"Yes, I'll miss him."

M.C.G.